CANO...
in a week

Sam Cook

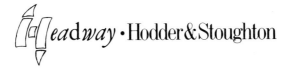
Headway · Hodder & Stoughton

ACKNOWLEDGEMENTS

The author would like to thank The British Canoe Union, Wild Water, Gaybo Limited, Avoncraft Limited, Out and About Limited, Bewerley Park Centre; the paddlers: the Liggins family, the Cass family, Lynn, Dan, Naomi, Sarah, Jenny and Martin, Alan Finer, the photographer and Val Bennison who typed the manuscript.

British Library Cataloguing in Publication Data
Cook, Sam
   Canoeing in a week. – (Sports in a week)
   I. Title   II. Series
   797.1

ISBN 0 340 55860 1

First published 1992

Typeset by Rowland Phototypesetting Limited, Bury St Edmunds, Suffolk. Printed in Hong Kong for the educational publishing division of Hodder and Stoughton Limited, Mill Road, Dunton Green, Sevenoaks, Kent by Colorcraft Limited.

CONTENTS

INTRODUCTION

A JOURNEY BY CANOE

The canoe is a vehicle of travel. From a very early time canoe-shaped craft have been the simplest and most basic form of travel by water. From the dug-out log of early civilisation to the birch bark canoe of the

INTRODUCTION

North American Indian to the sophisticated plastics of modern society, the canoe has remained a primitive but efficient vessel for water journeys. The canoe is silent. It glides through the water and leaves no trace. It has a special kind of freedom.

Some of the great explorers travelled by canoe and, in more modern times, the canoe has been the vehicle for some wonderfully adventurous expeditions to places all over the world, often inaccessible by any other form of transport.

I recently met two brothers, now over seventy years old, who had escaped to England from Belgium during the Second World War in a wood and canvas folding canoe. What a journey that must have been!

A close friend of mine, who is an auxiliary coastguard, decided to take up canoeing and within three years he had made the first coastal circumnavigation of mainland Britain.

Canoeing is a sport that can be enjoyed at all levels. It's fun, it's exhilarating, it helps keep you fit and it can appeal to all age groups. Wherever your horizons might be set, this book sets out to introduce its reader to making a journey by canoe. Somewhere close to your back door will be a canal, river, lake or coastline just waiting to be explored. But before you launch out into that unknown territory, there are a few skills and some knowledge that will help you to do it safely.

MONDAY

HOW TO BEGIN

Learning to canoe is more fun with other people. There are no short cuts to becoming competent, but learning the basic skills will be quicker and more enjoyable in a group, particularly if you have a competent canoeist to guide you; and it is sure to be safer. As a beginner **don't canoe alone**; three or four is a safe number.

Clubs

Most large towns have a canoe club and this would be a good starting point. The club may not be able to offer exactly what you need, but it will be able to give you advice about where to find it.

The sport of canoeing is very diverse. Your journey is not the only type of canoeing that is on offer. Individual clubs may specialise in different aspects of canoe-sport, from flat water racing to shooting exciting white water rapids or slalom canoeing, a form of competition on rapids. Surfing, sea kayaking and even canoe sailing are also different types of canoe-sport.

The activities of a club will be determined by the type of water readily available to it. We are looking for flat water touring which takes place on navigable rivers, lakes or canals.

Not all clubs will cater for beginners, so be careful not to be drawn into canoeing activities that might not interest you or that might put you off.

MONDAY

Courses

Beginners' courses in canoeing are quite common and offer the
opportunity to gain experience in the correct way and to prepare you for
your prospective journey with good technique and in safety.

You will find all beginners make the same mistakes, and you are sure to
be less inhibited and more willing to have a go when you see others
doing the same.

Learning to canoe is all about experimenting with your paddle and your
canoe. Be prepared to try different ideas, play games, learn from each
other. Some canoes are best paddled by two people. The team work
involved can be very rewarding as well as giving you someone else to
blame when things go wrong. It will certainly help if you have an
experienced canoeist to teach you. These people are usually called
Instructors. Where can you find one?

The British Canoe Union

The British Canoe Union (BCU) at West Bridgford, Nottingham is the
national body for canoeing in Britain. The BCU knows all the canoe clubs
in the country and will have a register of all the centres and schools that
offer courses for beginners. It will be able to put you in touch with local
canoeists in your area who have similar interests to you.

Choosing a canoe

You will soon discover that there are a multitude of different types of
canoe, each designed specifically for its particular use. Even now, new
canoes are still being designed and new aspects of canoe-sport
developed. Canoes vary in price and quality. You may wish to hire a
canoe before you buy one. Second-hand canoes can be good value.
Canoeing magazines invariably have classified private sale
advertisements, which may be worth a look.

Before we go any further we need to determine some fundamental
terminology if we are to understand the difference between canoes and
kayaks.

Canoe A canoe is a boat which is propelled by a paddle with a single
blade. There may be one, two or more paddlers, but each will have a
single-bladed paddle. An example is the open canoe which originated in
North America. The canoe can also be covered with a deck. It is normal
for the paddler to sit in a kneeling position.

Kayak A kayak is propelled by a double-bladed paddle. It has a
covered deck inside which the paddler sits. The cockpit can be large,
where it is easy for the paddler to fall out if the kayak should capsize, or

From left to right: Swimming pool canoe; White water tourer; Sea canoe; Flat water touring canoe; General purpose canoe. Bottom: Open touring canoe

small, where it is intended to give the paddler a good grip with the knees for use in rough water. Again, these are built for one, two or more paddlers.

Technically, the paddlers would be called canoeists or kayakists. Collectively, they are called canoeists. The boats we will call canoes. Where it is necessary to differentiate, we will call them open canoes or kayaks.

For the beginner, a general purpose or touring canoe is ideal. You can see examples in the picture. Using one of these will make the skills necessary for your journey easier to manage. An open canoe will be easier to handle with two paddlers.

We will talk more about other factors in the choice of canoe later in the book.

What to wear

Assuming your introduction to canoeing is during the summer, it is not essential to use expensive specialist gear. Normal clothing like tracksuits, lightweight trousers and sweaters or fibrepile is adequate. A few thin layers of clothing are better than one thick layer. This will give better insulation, and you can peel off layers or add them, depending on your preference. You will need more than just a pair of shorts on all but the hottest of days.

A wind and waterproof lightweight top garment will be necessary even in the summer. If you are wet, it will help prevent you from becoming chilled. Even in a light breeze you will soon cool down.

Keep warm. Try and maintain a comfortably warm body temperature. Getting cold can become serious apart from interrupting your enjoyment.

Never go afloat without footwear; training shoes are ideal. You never know what is below the surface of the water, and stubbing your toe on a rock or piece of equipment can be very painful. Avoid heavy footwear like boots.

When you have more experience you may decide to buy some clothing designed for canoeing. See what other canoeists are wearing and seek advice from them.

Take a change of clothes with you and learn how to waterproof them so that they can go in the canoe with you. More about this in Saturday's chapter.

Buoyancy aids

A buoyancy aid is essential; always wear one when canoeing. If you are on a course it will be provided for you, together with the other

MONDAY

equipment. If you are buying one, take advice from other canoeists or the shop assistant. This is one piece of equipment where it is not always wise to buy the cheapest. It should be a snug fit and conform to European safety standards. It will also help to keep you warm and give protection to your upper body.

A cautionary note about swimming ability

It is common practice for anyone pursuing water activities to be able to swim. In reality, it is your confidence in the water that is important, particular in getting your head wet. Your buoyancy aid will keep you afloat. If you are unable to swim, or lack confidence in the water, start your canoeing activities in a swimming pool with a canoeist who can show you what to do. It will help your swimming and give you the confidence necessary to enjoy your canoeing.

Transporting and carrying equipment

Canoes and kayaks are easily transported. This is one of the great advantages over other boating activities. Transporting equipment does, however, require care. Equipment can become damaged or, more seriously, can cause an accident.

MONDAY

Ensuring that your equipment is stacked and secured firmly is a skill worth learning. It is common sense really, but here are a few points to consider.

A safe load

Nylon webbing with buckle – the easiest and safest method of tying on

MONDAY

- Be sure your roof rack is sturdy enough for the job.
- Space the roof rack as widely as possible on the roof.
- Use good quality straps and ropes for tying on and replace when there are any signs of wear or fraying. Avoid elastic bungies.
- Tie down to front and rear of the vehicle as well as the sides.
- Avoid overloading. It is possible to carry 3–4 kayaks on a good rack.
- Use a roof rack with a locking device so that it is attached to the vehicle for security.
- If left unattended, lock your canoe to the roof rack. Use a wire and padlock like a bicycle lock.
- Avoid carrying equipment inside the canoe. It will possibly increase the load to an unsafe weight, and either fall out during the journey or disappear with a light-fingered passer-by.
- Avoid getting water inside the canoe; this can add a lot of weight to the roof load. Stack the canoes upside down or cover the cockpits with a fitted apron.

Working together to load and unload

MONDAY

Carrying the canoe

Care is also important when carrying your canoe on or off the vehicle and down to the water. Look after your boat and look after your back. Learn good lifting techniques.

Using the knees to aid lifting

It is always easier to work with a partner and help each other.

MONDAY

The paddle

Finally, before going afloat, you will find it useful to practise using your paddle or simulating a paddling action on the land. This is not essential, but may save you some time when sat in your canoe trying to work it out.

Length and grip of paddle   The picture indicates the ideal length for your paddle and where to put your hands.

Holding the paddle   Place your hands a comfortable distance apart – just outside the width of your shoulders would be ideal. Learn to hold the paddle away from your body with your almost straight.

The top of the open canoe paddle has a handle to grip. Your fingers curl over the top with your thumb underneath.

The kayak paddle is held with the hands at equal distance from the centre. The blades are **feathered** which means they are set at an angle

The control hand holds the paddle blade at the correct angle

to each other, usually 90 degrees. This reduces wind resistance on the blade not in the water. The paddle must rotate between alternate blades entering the water.

This rotation is controlled by one hand, either your left or right. You will have to experiment to decide which is the natural hand to control the rotation. This hand will hold the paddle firmly whilst the other hand will have a loose grip.

The kayak blade can be flat or curved. Paddles with curved blades will be constructed for either left or right hand control.

Like canoes, there is a large selection of paddles designed for different uses (see Tuesday's chapter for diagrams of different paddles). If you are buying, seek advice from the shop on a suitable paddle for touring. The price, which can range from £20–£80, will reflect the quality of the paddle.

Now practise moving your paddle through the air to get the feel of it. Sit on the bank at the edge of the water. Pull the blade through the water so you can feel how the blade should be full face to the pull.

UNDERSTANDING TERMINOLOGY

The boat

The two drawings will give you most of the names with which you should become familiar. Some are common to any type of boat.

Kayak

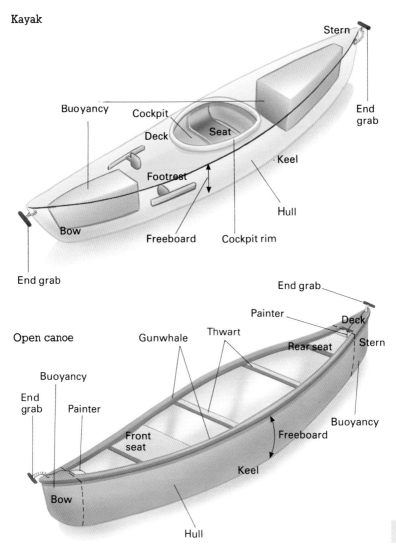

TUESDAY

Certain parts of your canoe are important for safe canoeing. It should, of course, be watertight, or seaworthy, as it is sometimes called.

Buoyancy   Your canoe must float if it becomes waterlogged. This is achieved by buoyancy built into the construction. Kayaks usually have polyethylene foam blocks fixed in place – these are important for structural strength as well. Open canoes may also have foam blocks. Some new plastic hulls are made from a sandwich construction with buoyancy in the sandwich. The buoyancy must be evenly distributed so the canoe floats horizontally when waterlogged. The minimum recommended quantity of built-in buoyancy is 30 kilograms. It can be increased easily by using inflatable airbags. This is a good idea because more buoyancy increases the safety by further reducing the quantity of water that can fill the canoe. This also helps considerably when emptying out after a capsize.

End grabs   These are essential at the bow (front) and stern (back). Fibreglass or plastic is slippery when wet, and difficult to hold. A toggle is the safest and most practical fitment to use. Avoid loops into which your fingers could be trapped.

Cockpit and seats   There should be no loose ropes or equipment around this area. The last thing you want is to get caught up when you are making a quick exit. The seat should be comfortable. Try it out before launching.

Footrest   In a kayak it is important to have a footrest. If properly adjusted, it will improve your paddling performance. The footrest must be designed not to trap your feet should you either slide past it or twist sideways before you exit during a capsize. Most modern kayaks have footrests designed to be safe. Some straight-running kayaks are fitted with rudders. The rudder is controlled by the feet. The fitments should not cause any obstruction.

Splash-deck   This is a skirt that fits around your body and around the cockpit of a kayak. Its purpose is to prevent water from splashing into the cockpit. Wearing a splash-deck is unnecessary for initial training. When you do decide to wear one, be sure to practise removing it from the cockpit so that it does not present a problem if you capsize. A warm swimming pool is a good place to practise. The splash-deck must be fitted with a secure release tab.

TUESDAY

Paddle This is the name for the whole item. The central bar that is held is called the loom or shaft. On the end of the shaft are the blades. The blades have a reverse face and a drive face. The open canoe paddle has a handle at one end of the shaft.

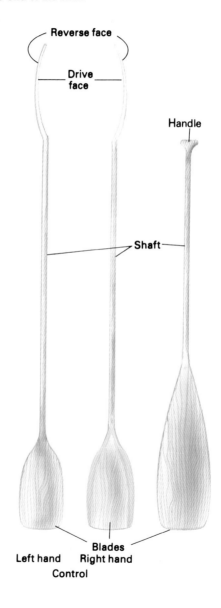

Reverse face

Drive face

Handle

Shaft

Blades
Left hand   Right hand
Control

TUESDAY

Launching

So! The time has come to get on the water. How you do this will depend on your confidence. The launch in the picture is probably too extreme for your first try!

First, check your buoyancy aid is fastened correctly. Choose a section of bank that is no higher than your canoe, and free from obstructions. Lift the canoe into the water and be sure it is floating freely.

You will find it useful to work with a partner, who can help both with lifting the canoe and steadying it whilst you climb in.

Launching an open canoe – working together

There are several different methods of entry.

Using the paddle as an outrigger is the most stable and will help you initially. Climbing in and out of your canoe is the most likely time to get wet.

▶ *This method is useful when the bank is higher than the canoe*

TUESDAY

Keep a firm grip on the bank whilst pulling the canoe towards it. With one foot in the canoe, move your weight from the bank to the centre balance point of the canoe in one single movement. The results of not making this move confidently are obvious.

Whoops!

It is good practice to try a few different methods. It will improve your balance and prepare you for when the bank is not at a convenient height. You will soon learn to have fun launching.

Sitting

In a kayak it is obvious that you have to sit, but a balanced, comfortable position is important for your posture and your paddling. The footrest should be adjusted so that your knees are bent to just below the deck. Now stretch your upper body and avoid leaning backwards.

Sitting or kneeling is a choice in the open canoe. Kneeling, with your backside resting against the seat, is more stable and will give you a more dynamic paddling position. Try this first.

When your knees or ankles become tired sit up on the seat, or with one knee up and one down.

Kneeling

One knee

Sitting

TUESDAY

Moving away from the bank

Your use of the paddle will be limited at this stage, so gently push away from the bank with your hand or your paddle. Your canoe needs to move sideways sufficiently for you to paddle between the bank and the canoe. If the bow is turned away from the bank more than the stern, you will be able to paddle away more easily. Soon you will learn a stroke to help you move sideways.

Forward paddling

You have already practised with your paddle on the bank, so the forward paddling action will be familiar to you. It will be slow and unrhythmical at first, but feeling the canoe move through the water will be exhilarating.

Forward paddling

During the stroke, the kayak paddle should be approximately 45 degrees to the horizontal. The open canoe paddle should be almost vertical with one hand directly above the other. Forward paddling is a skill that will take many hours of practice to perfect. Don't expect to be an expert immediately.

Blade square to the canoe

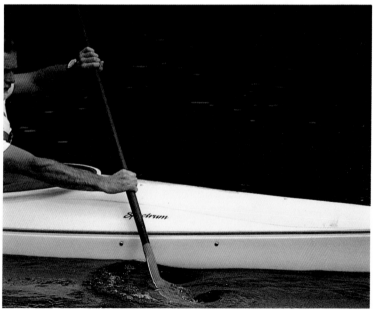

Blade square to the canoe

TUESDAY

Here are a few pointers to help you.

Technique Tips – Forward paddling

- Sit tall and relax your body.
- Look straight ahead.
- Hold the paddle away from your body with the upper arm at shoulder height.

Hold the paddle away from the body

- Check your grip of the paddle – width and control hand.
- Punch forward with your upper arm and shoulder and draw back with the lower.
- Keep the blade square to the side of the canoe.

Steering

At this early stage, you will experience some difficulty with steering your canoe or making it go where you want it to go. This is called **directional stability**.

If a rudder is fitted, you will be learning how to control it with your feet. The rudder should then control the direction in which you travel. In all other canoes the paddle is your rudder. In time, your forward paddling will improve and direction will be maintained with small adjustments in the paddling stroke. As a beginner, you may need to adopt a more direct approach.

Once the canoe has veered off course, you will need to counteract with a rudder stroke at the stern of your canoe.

If the canoe veers right – rudder on the left. If the canoe veers left – rudder on the right. In the open canoe this will require changing sides with the paddle. This stroke is called the **stern rudder**. It will only work effectively if the canoe is moving forwards.

Using the paddle as a rudder

If you slow down or stop, more sideways pressure on the blade will be necessary.

Technique Tips – Stern rudder

- Hold the paddle with your normal hand grip.
- Keeping the arms almost straight, turn the shoulders so that the paddle is almost parallel with the length of the canoe.
- Keep the top hand low – about stomach height.
- The paddle blade should be vertical in the water with the drive face towards the canoe. Control this with your wrists.
- Push out sideways, with the reverse face, and resist the water pressure on the blade.

The paddle in position for stern rudder

If you are paddling with a partner in either kayak or open canoe, the heavier person in the rear seat position will make steering easier, and it will be this paddler who has most control over steering.

TUESDAY

Returning and coming ashore

Using forward paddling and the stern rudder, you should be able to turn around and head back to your launching area.

Coming ashore requires careful judgement of speed and direction. Paddle diagonally towards the bank, then use the stern rudder to glide in and steer your canoe to a stop alongside the launching position.

If you misjudge it, don't lunge for the bank with your body; you could find yourself in the water. Just paddle away and try again. You will certainly appreciate why you need a clear, obstruction-free launching area.

Exit from the canoe is a reverse of launching. Work with a partner until you are confident. Your partner, however, is only there to hold your canoe steady to the bank; learn to climb out on your own.

Weather and its effect on canoeing

Canoeing is such a diverse sport, with all its various aspects, that it is possible to go canoeing in almost any weather conditions. As a beginner to the sport, however, you will need to be cautious about certain weather conditions.

Sun

It is always more pleasant to canoe when the sun is shining, but, in Britain, if you wait for the sun to come out you will rarely put your canoe on the water.

Occasionally, however, we do experience heatwave conditions. On the water, the effect of ultra-violet rays from the sun is more intense. The reflection off the water is similar to the reflection off the snow when skiing. It can quickly be harmful to the skin and the eyes, so be safe and cover up.

Wind

Wind is an element of the weather that one would not associate as a hazard to canoeing. In fact, it would take a surprisingly strong wind before there is a danger of capsizing.

The wind, even a light breeze, does however have a dramatic effect on the directional stability of a canoe, particularly open canoes which have more freeboard than kayaks. (Freeboard – the height of the canoe out of the water.) We will learn later how to trim the boat to counteract this effect.

The wind can affect the speed at which you travel. A following wind will increase your speed, whilst a headwind may reduce your speed to almost a standstill.

TUESDAY

More serious is the effect of the wind on large open areas of water. This is where, with your limited experience, you must be cautious. Winds blowing away from the shore have the danger of also blowing you away. On-shore winds blowing across a sizeable lake may cause waves large enough to swamp or fill your canoe.

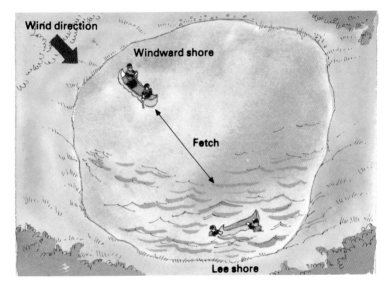

On tidal waters the waves may change a normally calm canoeing venue into a playground for the surf canoeist.

TUESDAY

Rainfall

Canoeing in the rain is not an unpleasant experience. As already mentioned, canoeing is less affected by normal weather conditions than most outdoor sports. Sensible canoeing clothing is obviously designed for the possibility of getting wet.

But, heavy continuous rainfall can present a danger to the canoeist. As we all know, rivers are susceptible to flooding. The white-water canoeist is excited merely by the thought of a flash flood. Many upland rivers are only negotiable when in spate conditions. For the inexperienced, however, caution is the prudent course. When the river turns brown, stay on the ground.

Weather forecasting

Information about the weather is readily available nowadays from several convenient sources.

Radio and television weather bulletins   These vary considerably in their detail. Particularly good are national and regional reports on breakfast television and at major news times during the day. Radio forecasts are comprehensive on Radio 4 at 6.55 a.m., 7.55 a.m., 12.55 p.m. and 17.55 p.m.

Telephone   Weathercall is a call service giving national and regional forecasts. The pre-recorded message is updated twice a day. It is a very convenient method of obtaining an up-to-date forecast. A handy pocket-size plastic card contains telephone numbers covering the whole of the United Kingdom. A similar telephone service – Marinecall – is specific to coastal forecasts and information on weather around the coast of the United Kingdom. Both plastic cards are available from Telephone Information Services Limited, Dewhurst House, London EC1A 9DL.

WEDNESDAY

DANGER AWARENESS

Canoeing is an adventure sport and will always carry an element of risk. Common sense and an awareness of the possible dangers and hazards should be sufficient to keep you out of trouble.

Don't be put off by this section of the book which highlights the possible hazards. Several thousand people go canoeing every year and the percentage of serious accidents is extremely small. Awareness and knowledge of the dangers will be a major factor in ensuring that you are always in control. Be alert and avoid your journey becoming an epic. Plan thoroughly and acquire the skills and knowledge necessary for your trip. **Be adventurous, but remember that your ambitions must match your abilities.**

Even with your limited experience so far, it would be possible to make a short journey along some sheltered water. Here are a few cautionary notes before you do.

River danger awareness

Weirs are a feature of most rivers in Britain. Where the river is a recognised navigation for boats, there are usually ample sign warnings about the approach of a weir, and an associated bypass channel with a lock.

Weirs do occur frequently on other rivers often with little or no warning of their approach.

A safe weir

The main reason they are a danger is because of the turbulent water pattern that is formed due to the sudden drop in height of the river bed.

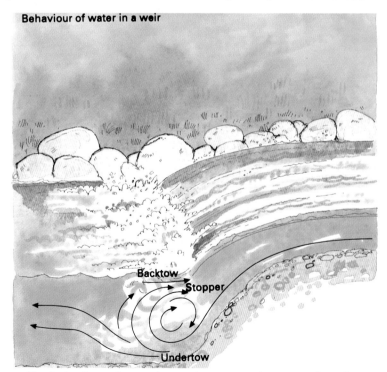

The behaviour of water in a weir causes a dangerous foaming wave

WEDNESDAY

Shooting a weir can be disastrous to your equipment

Although the general advice is to keep away from weirs, many of them are safe to canoe (shoot). Deciding whether or not a weir is safe to shoot requires intimate knowledge of the shape of the weir; the effect that this shape has on different volumes of water; the effect the water will have on your canoe, and you, should you end up in it.

It would take a whole book to explain all the different types and shapes of weir and the secrets they hold. Don't experiment on your own. If it looks safe to canoe, make sure you are with an experienced canoeist whose judgement you respect.

IF IN DOUBT, PORTAGE OUT.

Bridge stanchions   All obstacles built in the water should be treated with caution. They often erode leaving metal spikes and sharp-edged blocks. Where a river flows under a bridge, the water flow is often increased and a strong current is caused through the arches. Keep clear of the bridge supports as they are a collecting place for debris which may include you if you paddle too close.

WEDNESDAY

Bends   The current tends towards the outside of the river on a bend. Erosion occurs and the bank becomes a hazard. The safe, although slower, course is towards the inside of the bend.

Bank erosion

Trees   Trees overhanging the water can be a major hazard. A fallen tree in the water is even more dangerous as the water passing through it can suck you under. Fallen trees often appear on bends where the bank has eroded. Avoid trees at all costs.

Lining the canoe round a tree obstruction

Flooded rivers   Spate conditions occur more frequently during the winter months but flash floods from heavy storms can cause an alarming rise in the water level at any time of year. Rivers are canoeable in these conditions, but all the previously mentioned hazards become increasingly more dangerous due to the volume and speed of the water. Luckily, these conditions are predictable and are, therefore, easily avoided.

Special lake hazards

Wind   The major caution here is the effect of the wind as mentioned under Weather. Waves caused by the wind could capsize or swamp the canoe. (Swamp – water enters the canoe and waterlogs it.) The shoreline may be such a distance that swimming to shallow water is not practical. Some knowledge and practice in how to rescue an upturned canoe in deep water is essential. Attempting this on your own is extremely difficult, and is one good reason why you should be extremely cautious about canoeing alone. White-water paddlers and sea-kayakists learn to eskimo roll, the technique of self-righting the canoe after a capsize, but this is not possible in open canoes and kayaks with large cockpits.

Deep water rescues (see Friday, page 64) emphasise the need for maximum buoyancy in your canoe. This method of rescue is not possible with a canoe fully laden for an expedition.

Trim for wind   Facing the canoe directly into wind is the safe position to adopt if the wind presents a difficulty. You will feel more stable, and lessen the possibility of becoming swamped. Steering will become difficult in all directions except head to wind, and even this may not be easy in an open canoe.

To improve your directional stability it is possible to trim the canoe so that it is either bow or stern heavy. The least heavy end of the canoe will be blown downwind.

To travel upwind – load the bow.   To travel downwind – load the stern.

This is easily achieved in the open canoe – the paddlers move forwards or backwards.

Trim for wind

Be careful not to overload as this will increase the possibilities of swamping.

WEDNESDAY

The kayak, with its fixed seat position, allows little flexibility for altering the trim. Equipment inside the boat would have to be used. This change of trim could only take place before you leave the shore.

Other craft

The canoe is a relatively slow-moving boat. Other craft on the water may often be travelling much faster; sometimes at high speed. The wake left by fast-moving boats is not usually a problem, in fact, it can be fun on an otherwise calm day.

These are some of the hazards that are best avoided.

- The waterskier who may be carving a much larger arc than the speedboat towing the skier.
- The learner on a jet ski who may not be in complete control.
- The windsurfer surfing at high speed who seems to enjoy missing the canoe by inches.
- The fleet of racing yachts that may expect you to move out of their way.
- Although motorised craft should give way to non-motorised craft, it would be prudent for you to make a move before they plough through you. They may not see you.

Canals

Motorised craft frequent the canals. Although there is a speed limit, they are more than likely to be travelling faster than the canoe and may approach you from the opposite direction surprisingly fast.

THE RULE OF THE ROAD IS KEEP TO THE RIGHT

This is the opposite to driving on roads in the United Kingdom, and the same as driving on the continent.

Locks are normally portaged by canoe. This is usually quicker, and certainly less hazardous. If you decide to venture through a lock, keep away from the flooding end. Be careful not to be squeezed between two boats or between a boat and the lock walls, and hold onto the wall or another boat to keep stable. Probably a safer method is to tether your canoe from both ends whilst you control it from the bank.

Portaging is easier with a home-made trolley

Lining through a lock

It is much safer to go through an emptying lock (downhill) than a filling lock (uphill).

WEDNESDAY

Swans   Beware of large water fowl, like swans. They are very protective of their territory, particularly if they are mating or have young. They can be quite alarming if they decide to take off towards you. I have known canoeists to be knocked out of their boats by the wing tip of a swan. If in doubt, get out and line your canoe whilst you walk along the bank.

Another possible hazard for some of us along the network of canals that winds through our towns, cities and countryside, is the quantity of public houses that may be encountered. All things in moderation!!

Anglers

There is often conflict between boats and anglers. Fishing is one of the most popular pastimes. Boats, in general, disturb this activity. Anglers often cast their lines across the watercourse to the further bank, making it difficult to pass without interruption. The angler is often also well-camouflaged amongst the foliage of the bank, and may not be noticed until the last moment.

He has a right to be there, and the canoeist should make every effort to pass unobtrusively. You have the advantage over other boats in that your canoe travels silently and should give you the best opportunity to pass by with the minimum of disturbance.

Health hazards

Finally, a hazard that has been increasing in recent years is water pollution. Although canoeing is potentially a wet sport, it is prudent to be discerning about where it is pleasant or unpleasant to get wet.

Basic techniques

Turning

Turning can be achieved in several ways. You have already learnt that by **forward paddling** on one side and using a **stern rudder** on the other, the canoe can be turned round in a long, wide arc.

You may have discovered for yourself that you can turn in a tighter circle by using a **reverse stroke** instead of the stern rudder. A **reverse stroke** is similar to forward paddling, except that the stroke begins at the stern of your canoe and pushes towards the bow.

Using forward and reverse strokes, the canoe can be turned on the spot. Improving the efficiency of the turn can be easily achieved by using the **sweep stroke**.

WEDNESDAY

In the following picture sequence you will see that the paddle blade makes a wide, sweeping arc to increase turning momentum.

Technique Tips – Sweep strokes

Paddle
- Fully immerse the blade, keeping it square to the surface.
- The shaft should be low.
- The forward sweep arc should pull smoothly in a three-phase action.
    1) Out away from the bow.
    2) Parallel to the canoe.
    3) In, towards the stern.
- The reverse sweep should start at the stern and make a similar arc towards the bow. The reverse side of the blade pushes forward.

Your body
- Arms should be relatively straight throughout the stroke; the lower arm bending during phase 3.
- The shoulders rotate parallel with the paddle shaft, whilst the head looks in the direction you intend to travel. (In the learning stage, if you watch the blade in the water it will help you rotate.)
- Keep the upper arm lower than shoulder height.
- In the open canoe, extra leverage can be gained by leaning the body forwards and backwards during the stroke.

Practise the stroke from a stationary position, then learn how to use it whilst travelling forwards. This can be a useful stroke to help steering if you still have a problem in keeping a course.

Stopping

Sometimes it will be necessary to stop quickly. This is achieved by simply using short, quick reverse strokes.

The strokes are powerful, as you are counteracting the speed of the canoe. The intention is to maintain the same direction whilst stopping.

Technique Tips – Stopping

- Brace your legs firmly to keep control of the balance.
- The blade enters the water square to the surface, just behind the body, with the reverse side forward. Normal grip.
- In the kayak, alternate the strokes from side to side in quick succession. Only half submerge the blade on the first stroke, increasing the depth for the following three or four.
- The open canoe, paddled by a pair, will probably stop in a single, powerful stroke.
- Stopping as a single in an open canoe requires a contorted action of crossing the paddle to the opposite side on the second and fourth stroke. This requires good flexibility in the upper body, so be cautious to begin with.

WEDNESDAY

More power

Now you are beginning to use the paddle more effectively, it should be possible to increase power and speed in your forward paddling.

WEDNESDAY

Directional control is maintained by small adjustments to the paddle stroke.

Technique Tips – Forward paddling directional control – kayak

- Learn to anticipate direction of the bow so that you can counteract the possibility of moving off course before it happens.
- Look straight ahead and fix a target to aim for.
- Slight adjustments are made by:
  - increasing the speed of the blade through the water;
  - slight sweep out from the bow;
  - slight pull in at the stern. This is combined with a slight increase in the length of the stroke.

The sweep stroke will also have introduced you to rotation of the trunk. It is now time to build this into your forward paddling. It will help to increase power as you use the whole upper body, particularly the shoulders.

Use the whole lower body effectively by driving the force alternately through to your feet against a properly adjusted footrest.

Technique Tips – Forward Paddling, Rotation

- The shoulders should remain parallel with the paddle shaft.
- Keep arms straight, thrust forward with upper and draw back with lower.
- Keep blade close to the boat, except when correcting direction.
- Avoid letting the upper hand cross the mid-line of the kayak, except when correcting direction.
- Relax the hand in the thrust forward position and straighten the wrist.

You will develop your own style, and good technique will not only be efficient but effective in conserving energy.

The open canoe forward paddling stroke

Directional stability is maintained by using a rudder action at the end of the forward paddling stroke. This stroke is only used by the stern paddler or the solo paddler.

After the pull, the drive face of the blade is turned vertical to the surface and out away from the canoe. This turning movement is controlled by the hand and wrist on the handle. The blade is then pushed sideways away from the canoe. This is called the J stroke – the action prescribes the shape of a J.

Paddle path through the water

THURSDAY

PLANNING THE JOURNEY

A large part of the fun in making a journey is planning it and making sure that everything is thought about before you go. On a major expedition this is critical as your survival may depend on it. Be sure that everyone intending to make the journey is involved in the preparation; the whole group will then feel involved and committed to the venture.

Decide what preparation is required by making a list. Each person should then decide what they would like to be responsible for. Working in pairs is a good idea; it is a double check to avoid missing anything out.

Venues

Choosing a venue will depend on many factors. This is the most important decision to be made, upon which all else depends. Everybody should be involved. Consider the following points in your choice.

- How much time is available?
- How long is the journey to be – a day trip, overnight, or longer?
- Accessibility.
- Suitability for the paddlers.
- Is the venue dependent on weather conditions?
- Does the venue offer a natural objective

Information sources on venues:

- BCU
- Library
- British Waterways
- Canoeing magazines
- Other canoeists.

Transport logistics

Wherever your journey takes you, you will need transport. Getting to and from the venue should be relatively straightforward, with whatever transport is available to carry your equipment and team. Organising the transport from the start to the finish of the journey is the problem. Here are some possibilities:

- With two or more vehicles – unload all the equipment at the start. Drive all the vehicles to the finish; leave, and return to the start with all the drivers in one car.
- One vehicle and a non-canoeing driver who will collect you at the finish.

- One vehicle and public transport. Either leave the vehicle at the start and return to collect it via public transport at the end of the journey, **or** leave the vehicle at the finish and use public transport to return before starting the journey.

- One vehicle and another form of transport, like a bicycle. A similar system to public transport; this is only suitable for short distances and requires a secure place to leave the bicycle (although with open canoes it could be transported with you).

Whatever option you decide upon, it is worth informing somebody (possibly the police) of your plans, as a vehicle left overnight may cause concern, particularly as you may be seen leaving by canoe.

THURSDAY

First day paddling

Touring canoes travel at an approximate speed of four miles per hour. Fifteen to twenty miles will be a good day's paddle. The distance will depend on:

- Your fitness and stamina.
- The natural objectives of the journey.
- Location of places to stop for the night.
- The amount of sightseeing along the route.

Longer distances than this are obviously possible. At this early stage in your canoeing be cautious of an over-ambitious distance. You should avoid over-exerting the muscles, which will result in stiffness or strain.

It always takes longer than planned to get started on the first day, therefore a shorter distance is advisable. Allow time in your journey for exploring things of interest on the way, and also for unfavourable weather conditions, such as a headwind.

If you have energy for more canoeing at the end of the day, your planning has been sound. You will probably be in an unfamiliar place, and a short paddle after supper, or perhaps in the moonlight exploring your surroundings will be extremely satisfying, and only possible if you have not over-exerted yourself.

Maps and guides

It is difficult to actually be lost whilst following a watercourse such as a river or canal. However, not knowing exactly where you are will be frustrating and, possibly, confusing. A map or guide is an essential part of your equipment and should be accessible to look at whilst on the water. It will also give you information on:

- Access points – road information for transport.
- Distances.
- Campsites, Youth Hostels, Inns.
- Points of interest.
- Dangers: weirs.

The most suitable map is the Ordnance Survey Landranger Series Scale 1:50,000 available from bookshops and stationers. Some rivers have canoeing guides, and there are comprehensive guides to most canal networks. These are available from the BCU or British Waterways.

Your map should be weatherproofed; at least with a plastic bag. A hill-walker's map case is a good idea, or a more waterproof method is to sandwich it between clear sticky sheets of plastic. Highlight important features on the map before you cover it.

A selection of maps and guides

A waterproof map case

THURSDAY

Overnight stops

The one-day journey may be enough for you to contemplate at this stage, but I would encourage all canoeists to venture overnight. The experience encountered will be that special kind of freedom.

Canoeing and camping are aesthetically compatible. The weather is not always, but travelling under your own power, followed by a leisurely cooked meal and looking out at a magnificent sunset makes for all the other days when the weather may not be perfect.

It is not difficult to find campsites adjacent to the watercourses of Britain, but it may require some investigation and pre-planning.

The truly wild and natural campsites are few and far between. There is nothing more satisfying than cooking on an open fire, but you will have to search hard for this freedom on a campsite.

THURSDAY

Information sources on campsites:

- Maps and Guides.
- Local tourist information service.
- British Waterways Board.
- Yellow Pages telephone directory.
- Camping and Caravan Club.

Pre-book a campsite and, if possible, discover what facilities are available.

Alternative overnight accommodation could be:

- Youth Hostels.
- Bed and Breakfast – usually at farms or public houses.

Information sources would be:

- Local tourist information service.
- Telephone directory.

Places of interest

You will find your journey will be more enjoyable if you become fully aware of your surroundings as you pass through them. In the planning stages this can be helped by investigating places of interest.

Whilst you are canoeing, it is not always possible to be visually aware of the surroundings beyond the immediate banks of the watercourse, as they may be obscured by high banks or trees.

THURSDAY

Equipment, food and drink

Details of these items are all covered later in the book (see Saturday's chapter – pages 73–81). Planning needs to be thorough. Decide what is essential and what can be regarded as extras. You may be forced to abandon the extras if the weight or bulk become too great.

Access

In planning your journey you will need to seek advice on access to your chosen venue.

Access means

- Launching (access point).
- Passage of your canoe down the watercourse.
- Landing to leave the water (egress point).

The watercourse and adjacent banks will be privately owned. It is advisable to assume that you do not have a right of access, and to find out if canoeing is allowed.

Canoeing is not always welcome

Information – sources of access

The major source of information is through the BCU which operates a network of Local Access Officers from whom advice and information can be sought. You are more likely to receive a reply to your enquiry if you supply a stamped, self-addressed envelope.

Other sources include:

- British Waterways Board.
- Local Government Office – access land is often owned by the local council.
- Local canoeing clubs or activity centres.

You may find that a fee is charged for access.

A licence is necessary to canoe on British Waterways navigations. Membership of the BCU will include your licence fee.

Basic techniques

Moving sideways

When we first launched and moved away from the bank, we promised to learn the technique of moving sideways. You may have already discovered a way of doing this. It is great fun experimenting, so have a go at working things out for yourself.

The **draw stroke** is the name given to the basic stroke for moving sideways. The purpose is to fix the blade in the water and sideslip the canoe towards it. The position is the same for both open canoe and kayak. To start the stroke, reach out sideways then pull yourself towards the paddle. The drive face of the blade is towards the canoe and the shaft is held as vertical as possible.

Ready to start

Push-pull

End of draw

Slice back out

THURSDAY

After the sideslip, the power in the blade must be released so that your canoe does not trip over the paddle. It is easier at first to slice the blade out of the water and re-position it for another pull. A more proficient stroke involves twisting the blade through 90 degrees and slicing back out through the water. This action is made with the wrists.

Technique Tips – Draw stroke

- Attempt to keep the paddle vertical with the whole paddle on one side of the canoe.
- The blade enters the water as far from the boat as comfortable, and remains parallel to the canoe during sideslip.
- There is a push-pull action with the arms. The top arm should be no lower than the forehead, with the elbow pointing skyward – push. The lower arm extends out then – pulls – towards the hip, elbow towards the waist.
- Rotate the upper body and head towards the direction of travel.
- If the sideslip is not accurate, adjust the position of the blade fore or aft of the hip, to correct the sideways movement.

Draw stroke – open canoe

A draw stroke on the side that you normally paddle is the same as in the kayak. If you wish to move sideways in the opposite direction (e.g. moving left if you paddle on the right), you have a choice:

- Swap sides with your paddle. This is technically the easiest of the options – but not for the purist.

- Pry. This is a stroke unique to the open canoe. The paddle is held vertical as in the draw stroke. The blade is forced away from the canoe by leverage on the gunwhale.

Stern paddler using a pry

Technique Tips – Pry

- Begin the stroke with the blade underneath the canoe.
- Brace with your legs for stability.
- Take care not to hit an obstacle with the blade. You can produce enough leverage to break the paddle.
- The lower hand holds the shaft and the gunwhale. The top arm pulls to lever the blade out.
- The drive face of the blade faces the canoe as in the draw stroke.
- Return for another pry by twisting through 90 degrees and slicing back to the start.

THURSDAY

With two paddlers in the open canoe, to move sideways, one uses a pry whilst the other uses a draw.

The draw and pry strokes are also used whilst moving forward. Once you have reasonable control with the strokes try using them on the move. You will discover that by angling the leading edge of the blade away from the canoe, the stroke is more effective (with the pry, the leading edge is angled in).

Bow pry – stern draw

Moving backwards

Paddling in reverse is used for manoeuvring and slowing down.

The arm action and body movement have already been used in reverse sweep strokes and stopping. Developing the action into the **reverse paddling stroke** will be a natural progression.

Maintaining directional control can initially be effected with a reverse sweep or a rudder action at the bow.

A reverse J stroke is the skill required for moving backwards in the open canoe. The bow paddler has most control of the direction.

Technique Tips – Reverse paddling

- Normal grip on paddle. Use reverse of blade to push.
- Rotate the upper body to initiate the stroke so that the paddle shaft is almost parallel to the canoe.
- Look where you are going during body rotation.
- Keep the blade close to the side of the canoe unless sweeping out for steering.

FRIDAY

WHAT TO DO WHEN THINGS GO WRONG!

If we consider what could go wrong, the possibilities are endless – from a minor cut on the foot due to wearing inadequate footwear to a serious accident of drowning, from a breakdown in the transport arrangements to a broken canoe as a result of a capsize above a weir.

It is important to have a positive approach. All accidents or mishaps are avoidable by common sense precautions. Sound practice is a result of knowledge, suitable equipment, adequate training, and thorough planning.

Common sense rules

The common sense rules are:

Swimming ability   All paddlers should be able to swim in their canoeing clothing. It is not necessary to swim vast distances, but confidence in and under the water is essential. This confidence can easily be developed in safe and controlled surroundings, for example, in a swimming pool.

Personal flotation aid   Always wear your buoyancy aid when on or near the water. It would be foolish to take it off and then trip and fall into a lock whilst lining your canoe from the bank, or to jump in your canoe to rescue another capsized paddler and put yourself at risk having left your flotation on the bank. Be sure that the method of attachment is secure, and that the jacket is the correct size for the paddler.

'Fewer than three there should never be'   On the water, a minimum of two canoes is necessary, to enable one to rescue the other following a capsize. If you are involved in an accident, one paddler can attend to the injured paddler, whilst the third goes for assistance. This is the theory! If you paddle with less, you have to assess the potential risk. For example, is there a risk of capsize and, if so, how will you cope without any assistance?

Knowledge and experience   Be aware of your own experience, physical and mental capability, and that of your equipment; it will have limitations. Knowing what you, your partners and your equipment are capable of is the first key to avoiding the impossible. Like road traffic accidents, the cause has always been an error of judgement.

This is not to say that you shouldn't be adventurous. If your journey is successful and fills you with a feeling of exhilaration and fulfilment, you have had an adventure. If you return with a feeling of trepidation and fear as a result of a near miss or an epic, you will have experienced a misadventure. Only luck, and not your skill, will have allowed you to survive.

FRIDAY

Coping with a capsize

By the time this happens accidentally you will probably have practised, so the routine should be automatic.

- Stay calm.
- If you are paddling with a partner, check that they are safe.
- Stay with your boat, unless this will result in greater danger, e.g. a tree entanglement.
- Make your way to the bank, if practical. If not, signal to your team for assistance.

If coping with capsize is a skill that fills you with some trepidation, then choose the swimming pool as the most user-friendly venue initially to practise. If this is not possible, the natural environment will be OK – after all, this is where it might happen accidentally. Waist-deep water is sufficient for practice, and only a metre or two from the bank.

It is also useful to have someone standing by should you panic, or at least to help you empty the canoe.

Wear your buoyancy aid so that the practice is made as realistic as possible. If you intend using a splashdeck, this must also be worn, but not until you are confident capsizing without it.

FRIDAY

Technique Tips – Capsize

- Go for a swim first to accustom yourself to the water temperature.
- In the open canoe and large cockpit kayak you will simply fall out, possibly even keeping your hair dry; where the kayak cockpit is smaller and more restricting around the legs, a more definite push will be necessary to release yourself from the canoe.
- In the kayak, your body movement should simulate a forward roll action, upside down. This is best achieved by ducking your head towards the cockpit front. Place your hands behind you and push on the cockpit rim.
- Exit from the canoe before going for the surface with your head. Yes! you do have to hold your breath!

FRIDAY

Technique Tips – Capsize – *cont.*

- When you feel confident, try keeping hold of your paddle so that there is no chance of it floating away.
- Avoid leaning back or attempting to push your head to the surface before exit as this will create more difficulty in releasing your legs.
- Stay calm and relax.

Once out of your boat

- Check that your partner is safe if you are a double.
- Keep hold of the canoe and swim to the end where you can hold the end grab. If you are in a current, be sure to hold the upstream end. This is the safe position and avoids the possibility of you becoming trapped between your canoe and any obstacles in the water.
- The canoe should remain upside down. It will have trapped air inside, giving it additional buoyancy.
- Tow your canoe to the nearest shore. Hold the end grab and paddle in one hand, leaving the other free to help you swim. Swim on your back.
- Stay with your canoe; it will make you more visible and gives you additional buoyancy. Also, your canoe is more easily resued by another canoeist if you are still holding it.
- If you are drifting towards a danger, like a weir or overhanging trees, you may need to abandon the canoe for your own safety. The middle of a lake, however, is not the place to ditch your canoe and swim for the shore.
- If you do leave your canoe and are unable to retrieve it, be sure to inform the police. Finding an abandoned canoe may initiate a search by the authorities for the canoeist.

A word of encouragement

Getting wet is an experience that can usually be avoided. If capsizing will deter you from canoeing, you must choose equipment that is stable and unrestrictive. Your choice of venue and weather conditions will also reflect your reluctance to get wet. Before your journey, practise the skills that will give you confidence to avoid that inadvertent capsize.

Rescue of another canoeist

There are two simple methods of rescue for the flat water touring canoeist.

- Tow into shallow water.
- Deep water rescue.

FRIDAY

Tow rescue

Technique Tips – Tow rescue

- The swimmer is towed by holding onto the stern of the rescue canoe.
- Assess that it will be safe for you to effect a tow, e.g. no danger to the rescuer.
- Approach the capsize cautiously. Check that the swimmer(s) is OK and in a state ready to be towed. Don't allow panicking swimmers to grab your canoe.
- The swimmer should hold both canoes, forming a link between the two. Tow into shallow water; choose an area of bank where there are no obstructions.
- Do not attach yourself to the upturned canoe unless you have a properly designed tow line and you know how to use it.

This rescue is suitable on slow-moving rivers and canals.

FRIDAY

Deep water rescue
This is a more difficult rescue and requires some practice. The basic idea is for the rescuer to empty the upturned canoe, turn it the right way up, and assist the swimmer to re-enter the canoe. There are several different methods of deep water rescue. This method is called an X rescue. The photographs show the sequence of events.

FRIDAY

Technique Tips – Deep water rescue

- Approach the upturned canoe at the same end as the swimmer.
- Always keep the swimmer in sight and in contact with the canoes.
- The initial lift of the upturned canoe onto the rescuer's deck is difficult, but once the rescuer has hold of the canoe it acts like an outrigger and gives the rescuer stability.
- If more stability is needed, use the swimmer as a counter-balance on the opposite side.
- Once the canoe is across the deck in the X position, sufficient water should have emptied to complete the rescue.
- Float the canoes alongside each other to make a raft for the swimmer to re-enter.
- Re-entry in kayaks will be easier between the kayaks. Notice that they face in opposite directions and the swimmer is lying back.
- Re-enter an open canoe over the outside gunwhale. Assistance can be given by the rescuer.
- Take care not to lose the paddles during rescue. Kayak rescuers keep their paddle tucked into the waist.

If the canoes are loaded with equipment, it may be necessary to unload in order to effect an X rescue.

An alternative is to make a raft – turn the canoe upright – re-enter – and bail the water out.

If you are unstable and in danger of capsizing again, remain in a raft and make your way to the shore together. It will be slow but, hopefully, you will get there safely.

Medical problems

Some knowledge of medical conditions that could be a result of canoeing activity will be useful. It will help you in your common sense avoidance of problems.

Hypothermia

This is the medical term for exposure, the severe chilling of the body, and can result in death in a surprisingly short space of time.

The human body chills as a result of:

- immersion in cold water;

- wind chill – cooling of the body as a result of the wind;
- exhaustion;

or a combination of these factors.

Avoiding the possibility of this condition can be achieved by wearing clothes with good insulating properties, particularly windproof outer garments, eating plenty of high energy food, and not burning up all your energy by over-exertion.

Treatment of a paddler who has become hypothermic is achieved by preventing any further heat loss.

- Cease any further activity.
- Lie horizontally with the head slightly down so that the blood flows easily to the head.
- Insulate by whatever means available, e.g. more clothing, sleeping bag, tent or plastic bags.
- Reassure.
- Seek medical help.

Treating a casualty

FRIDAY

Drowning

The cause of drowning is pretty obvious. Asphyxia has occurred due to water entering the body via the mouth and nostrils and, usually, into the lungs.

In normal canoeing activity, and providing that buoyancy aids are worn, the danger from drowning is almost eliminated. However, the ability to save a life if it does occur is vitally important.

The first priority is to restore breathing and heartbeat. This involves Expired Air Resuscitation (EAR) and External Chest Compression (ECC). For more detail and training on this it is necessary to refer to a First Aid Manual and attend a First Aid Course.

Details of courses can be obtained from:

- British Red Cross Society
- St John's Ambulance Brigade

Contact addresses for these will be available at your local library.

Avoidance of accidents involving drowning is a result of good common sense canoeing but, if it does happen, don't be caught out not knowing what to do!

Weil's disease

Weil's disease is an infection caused by bacteria carried in rat's urine. It can be found in any water, but is more likely to contaminate stagnant or slow-moving waterways. The disease is a notifiable illness. It is rare, but serious, and requires hospital treatment. The bacteria is contracted through cuts and scratches, and through the mouth and nose into the bloodstream.

Common symptoms are:

- high temperature
- an influenza-like illness
- joint and muscle pains.

Let your doctor know that you have been canoeing. He/she should arrange a blood test.

Tendon strain

The wrists are a common strain area for the canoeist. A condition known as tenosynovitis, where the wrist tendons become inflamed, requires complete rest of the affected area. The condition can usually be avoided by good paddling technique, and reducing wrist movement when forward paddling.

Obviously, many other medical conditions can occur whilst canoeing, but not necessarily as a result of the activity. First aid knowledge gained through attending a course could be invaluable.

FRIDAY

First aid kit

What you carry in a first aid kit depends to a large extent on how much you know about using it.

It is usually possible to improvise with items like slings and bandages. You should probably carry a minimum of:

- Plasters (waterproof if possible) – for minor cuts, scratches, blisters.
- Large sterile dressings – for larger cuts or abrasions.
- Crepe bandages – for strains or support, wound strapping and improvised support bandage.
- Knife – for cutting anything from clothing, bandages, rope, etc.

Recovery position

Wherever an incident results in an unconscious casualty, more lives are saved by simply maintaining an open airway than any other treatment.

To achieve an open airway, place the casualty in the recovery position. This prevents any blood or fluid seeping down the throat.

AN UNCONSCIOUS CASUALTY SHOULD NOT BE LEFT UNATTENDED.

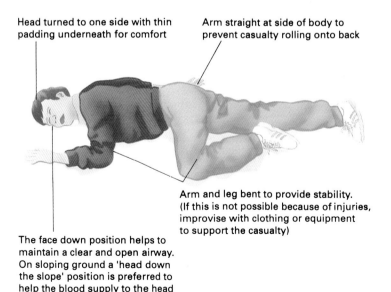

Head turned to one side with thin padding underneath for comfort

Arm straight at side of body to prevent casualty rolling onto back

Arm and leg bent to provide stability. (If this is not possible because of injuries, improvise with clothing or equipment to support the casualty)

The face down position helps to maintain a clear and open airway. On sloping ground a 'head down the slope' position is preferred to help the blood supply to the head

The recovery position

FRIDAY

Equipment repairs

Damage to your equipment is more likely than damage to a paddler, so it is important to be prepared for this.

You may need to be a little inventive sometimes when repairs are necessary. The two most serious will be a leaking canoe or a broken paddle.

Consider carrying the following items as a minimum repair kit for your journey:

- PVC plastic tape, 50 mm wide.
- Heavy gauge plastic sheeting, 1 metre square.
- Length of rope, 3–4 metres long, 2–4 mm thick.
- Knife.

Basic techniques

We have now arrived at the final stroke to give you basic control of your canoe. We have talked much about capsize, rescues and problems that may arise. This stroke is intended to prevent you from falling in the water.

The recovery stroke

For the stroke to be effective, it has to become a reflex action whenver your canoe reaches that point of no return and you join the fish!

FRIDAY

There are two positions for this stroke – High or Low.

Technique Tips – Low recovery

- The whole paddle is held low across the deck.
- Reverse side of the blade is placed flat on the water surface.
- Press down on the blade with the arms and upper body. The elbows are above the paddle.
- Apply pressure with the knee on the recovery side and flick the lower body upwards to recover the canoe.

> **Technique Tips** – High recovery
>
> - The whole paddle is held high, with the upper arm above eye height, elbows below the paddle.
> - The drive face of the paddle is towards the canoe and well out from the side.
> - Apply pressure with the recovery knee and flick the lower body up towards the paddle.
> - The paddle pulls down and in towards the canoe.

Capsize is likely whilst practising this stroke. It needs to be tested to its limit.

SATURDAY

THE JOURNEY

We are now approaching the time when your learning and practice can be put to the test. The journey is about to begin. This chapter completes your planning with information on: what to take with you; how this should be packed into your canoe; equipment and tips on camping; suggestions on food and drink.

If you are venturing on a day journey, not all the information will be relevant. If you are going the full distance – good luck – I think this section will help you on your way and increase your confidence.

What should I take?

The equipment you carry will essentially be the same for one night as it would be for a month. The obvious exception is the quantity of food. I have assumed the overnight stop to be camping. If your creature comforts determine that you arrange alternative overnight accommodation, then again all equipment and information will not be relevant. However, whether day tripping, camping or otherwise, you do need to consider equipment for emergencies, so we will consider this first.

Emergency kit

Shelter   Equipment to completely weatherproof a casualty is essential. A body-sized polythene bag is simple and unsophisticated. They are easily obtainable from camping shops. Some shelter for the whole party is desirable.

Insulation   Warmth is also essential. Spare clothing is the bare minimum. A sleeping bag and camping mat are ideal.

Sustenance   Providing a hot, sweet drink, though not essential, is desirable; it is a great morale booster. Unbreakable vacuum flasks are readily available and well worth the additional expense. If you are camping, you will have a cooking stove already. This drink should be in addition to your lunchtime drink.

High energy food should also be carried. Food and drink is not recommended as First Aid treatment, except in cases of hypothermia, where it could be life-saving. The rest of the party may need sustenance. If all goes well, chocolate bars are a special bonus to look foward to at the end of the journey.

First Aid Kit and Repair Kit   The contents of these two items are discussed in Chapter 5.

SATURDAY

Evacuation points   Pre-planned information on access points, telephones and road accessibility is a useful addition to your emergency kit.

Spare paddles   Like the mountaineer who loses his ice axe, the canoeist is somewhat hindered with a broken paddle. A spare paddle is a normal addition for the journey canoeist. The kayak paddle has a join in the shaft so it can be easily stowed.

Individual equipment

Clothing can be divided into wet and dry kit.

Wet kit is your canoeing clothing and should include some spares – at least an extra sweater. Actually getting wet is to be avoided on a journey, but remember, you will be using your wet kit for more than one day. Essentials are:

- Personal flotation aid.
- Full waterproof suit.
- Full clothing cover – All clothing should preferably have good insulation and quick-drying properties, e.g. fibre-pile garments.
- Suitable footwear.
- Some spare clothing.

Dry kit is your clothing to wear after landing, or in the event of an emergency. It must be kept dry at all costs. It should give you warmth and comfort after your exhausting paddle. Even though it should remain dry, quick-drying properties will be the best choice.

Comfort at night   Your sleeping bag is the most important piece of equipment to keep dry. There is a vast choice in the shops. Low bulk and good insulation are the factors that will determine your choice. A good idea is to have a bag that will keep you snug in the summer, and a fibre-pile liner to increase the insulation for colder times of year. A compression bag is useful to crush the sleeping bag smaller after packing.

SATURDAY

Most of the heat loss whilst sleeping out of doors is not through the air, but through the ground. An insulated mat is essential. These are made of foam, and also give a degree of comfort in ironing out the bumps where you lie.

Personal knick-knacks will include your washing kit, and extras like cameras, binoculars, money and valuables. What and how much you take will depend on many personal factors, not least your ability to pack up small and keep things dry.

Camping

Living out of doors has skills to be learnt, just like canoeing. Some of these skills can be rehearsed, such as tent pitching and lighting a stove. Others you will learn from experience. The more skilful you become, the more comfortable you will be. The skilful camper is as comfortable in the rain as when the sun shines. Learn to be organised.

SATURDAY

Campsites

Your choice of site may be restricted to established campsites due to the access of land alongside your waterway. Farmers, if approached sensitively, will often allow one-night camping at the edge of the water. If you are lucky, you may find a wilderness campsite, though even this may require permission.

Your requirements will be simple:

- A source of fresh water.
- Shelter from the elements.
- Level ground to sleep on.

Arriving at the end of the day, you will eventually develop your own routine, but here is a suggestion of what happens.

- Inspect the site, choose your spot, and erect your home for the night. Check that you are above any possible flood height.
- Make a brew; the canoe campers' refresher. I once spent twelve days in a Canadian wilderness park. After landing each evening, the first task was to light a fire, make a brew, and cook popcorn – a great revitaliser.
- Unpack and organise your home.
- Make your evening meal and relax.
- Explore the local area. A walk will be good for your legs after canoeing all day.
- Be sure to secure your canoe before retiring for the night.

The following morning, after enjoying a good breakfast:

- Pack up and stow all your kit.
- Dismantle your home last of all.
- Ensure there is no trace of your visit.

Camping equipment

If you are a backpacker, or you are familiar with lightweight carry on your back equipment, you will have a good starting point for choosing what you need for your night out.

The two main items are:

- Your home or tent.
- What you cook with.

Your home   There is a good selection of light/medium weight, 2/3 person tents on the market. The deciding factor will be the size and weight when packed in the canoe. A tent with a good size entrance verandah can be very useful if the weather drives you inside to prepare your meals. A family-size frame tent will be totally unsuitable for carrying in the canoe.

SATURDAY

There are alternatives to tents if you have that back to nature urge. The Bivvy can offer great flexibility and freedom. Beware of those midges; there is very little escape in the open air approach.

A makeshift shelter

An exciting alternative – a night on the water

Cooking equipment

The picture shows the choice in lightweight camping stoves.

From left to right: Top: Multi-fuel stove; Paraffin stove; Pressurised gas stove. Bottom: Nest of cooking pans; Petrol stove with pans; Meths stove with pans; Fuel containers

All are suitable and depend on personal preference. I use a methylated spirit stove It:

- is easy to light;
- works well in or out of the wind;
- is very compact as it contains its own cooking pans;
- is very stable;
- burns quietly.

All the stoves have disadvantages. The meths stove:

- has expensive fuel which is not always easily available;
- sometimes requires re-fuelling during cooking.

The choice is yours. Most stoves require the purchase of cooking pans separately. All except the gas stoves need a container to carry the fuel; this must be totally leak-proof. Leaking petrol, paraffin or meths will contaminate everything, as well as being an obvious fire hazard. Always keep the spare fuel away from the stove whilst cooking.

For safety reasons, it is preferable to cook at a distance from your shelter. Most stoves will require a windshield in order to work effectively. Whatever you use, make sure you are thoroughly familiar with its operation.

SATURDAY

The traditional canoe traveller will prefer to cook on an open fire. It fits the ethos of a simple nomadic existence. In the United Kingdom it is rare to find such a campsite. If you do, however, only use dead wood and, unless you find a permanent fire area, ensure there is no trace of the fire when you leave.

Besides your food, the pots and pans will be well-charred at the end of your meal! The modern, portable barbecue grill is a pleasant alternative. Always carry spare matches; they have a habit of getting damp.

SATURDAY

Included here is a suggested list of minimum camping equipment:

- Tent or shelter.
- Stove – fuel – matches – windshield.
- Cooking pans (minimum two) – lifting handle.
- Bowls – mugs – cutlery – sharp knife.
- Water container.
- Tin opener.
- Cleaning materials.

This list can be added to from personal preference.

Food and cooking

What influences your choice of food?

- Precise nutritional value of meals is not a significant factor. A one or two night journey is unlikely to result in scurvy!
- You will need food that provides plenty of energy. Quantity and calorific values are important. As a close friend of mine says, 'Keep the boiler stoked up.' A good-sized breakfast, nibbles through the day, and a hearty meal at night should be your aim.
- Fluid intake is also important. In warm weather, particularly, you will dehydrate; attempt to drink more than normal.
- Weight. If you load your canoe with tins, you will certainly travel more slowly, and it may affect your stability. Balance the weight with some lighter foods like pasta and cereal. Tins are waterproof, but when the labels come off, you have to play a guessing game.
- Bulk may not be too important for a one-night journey, but for longer excursions it will be a consideration. There are some tasty, compact lightweight packet foods on the market nowadays.
- Durability. Tomatoes, soft fruit and eggs don't travel too well. Bread can also be a problem; it's my favourite food, and difficult to do without. If you have an open fire or barbecue, you can always make unleavened bread; it's scrumptious! Just mix a stiff dough of flour, water and a pinch of salt. Twist the dough round a stick and bake on the embers. When brown, stuff the stick hole with jam and eat immediately. Preventing leakage of foods, like margarine or honey, is also a problem. Always pack them separately in as leak-proof a container as you can find.
- One pot meals. This does not mean the pot noodles variety. It means that your stove will only allow one pan of food to cook at a time, so stews are a better idea than meat and two separate vegetables.
- Cooking time. It may be necessary to use fuel sparingly. If so, choose quick cooking foods, e.g. three-minute pasta, corned beef.

Eating is important. On a journey, meals become your time clock. You are out there enjoying yourself, so indulge a little bit.

SATURDAY

The final word on camping is **cleanliness**. When living close to nature this is not just a matter of everyday hygiene like washing your hands, it also requires organisation around the camp site.

- Keep your water supply clean and well away from any toiletry.
- Cooking pans, and especially the lids, will be put on the ground, but keep the inside uppermost.
- Keep stove fuel well away from food.

On a six-week sea canoeing expedition in the Arctic, with food rations strictly limited, we had to eat paraffin-tasting porridge simply because we re-fuelled too near to the food. The re-fueller should not be the cook.

Packing

How can I waterproof my equipment?

Some suitable bags and containers are available from canoeing shops.

The most recent innovation of bags with a roll-down top and clip to fasten, is the most versatile for kayak and open canoe. The larger containers are only suitable for open canoes.

SATURDAY

A cheaper alternative is to make your own bags from waterproof material, or to use conventional polythene bags, e.g. bin liners or heavy gauge fertiliser bags. Sealing the opening is best achieved with rubber bands, e.g. an old vehicle inner tube cut into bands.

Sealing the bag with a rubber band

Sort out your equipment into groups. Only a percentage needs to be waterproof, e.g. sleeping bags, dry kit and food.

SATURDAY

Stowing the cargo

Here you will have to experiment. Find the most suitable arrangement for the equipment in your canoe. A few general principles:

- All equipment must be securely tied in.
- Avoid small, loose items. Put everything in bags.
- There should be no equipment around your sitting area, particularly ropes that may tangle with your legs.
- Balance and trim of your canoe is important. Stow heavier items near the centre.
- Some equipment will be needed during the day. Keep it handy.

SUNDAY

MORE TIPS FOR YOUR JOURNEY

At this final stage in the book, I could describe a particular journey example for you. This I have resisted because:

- It would be specific to a particular area of the country.
- Many aspects of your journey will be specific to your needs, e.g. distance travelled, type of canoes used, ages of the party, etc.
- Much of the fascination of canoe journeying is in discovering for yourself, finding out about and planning your journey.

Really, it is up to you to research and plan using the information given to you in the book. Your main sources of reference will be:

- The British Canoe Union.
- Local information services.
- Other canoeists.

There are endless classic journeys to be made on the major rivers and canal networks of the United Kingdom.

The more you investigate, the more excited I hope you will become about exploring in your canoe.

Here are a few more tips about considerations in your choice of venue.

Canals

- Portaging around locks is hard work. Look carefully at your map and check how many locks are on your route. You will be lucky not to have any, but think again if there seem to be a lot.
- Low swing bridges are also common. A small key can be purchased from canal shops. Opening swing bridges is good fun, especially with youngsters, and saves a lot of hard work carrying equipment.
- Don't dismiss canals that weave through cities or industrial areas. Apart from the dead prams and refrigerators, there is often fascinating industrial archaeology to be seen.

Rivers

- Rivers that are British waterways navigations will have less inherent dangers than more upland rivers, and will be a good choice for your first journey.
- When you are ready to move on to other rivers, be sure to check out all the available information on any difficulties you may encounter.
- Always be prepared to line or portage around hazards. If there is any doubt – portage out.

SUNDAY

Loaded for portage

Avoiding danger by wading

SUNDAY

Estuaries

- Be cautious of any tidal waters. Make sure you know how to calculate the tide.
- Seek local advice.
- You may well encounter fast currents. Your canoeing skills must be proficient.
- When an estuary dries out, it invariably leaves large expanses of deep mud on the banks. These are to be avoided.

Coastal waters

- What might appear to be inviting water is likely to have many hidden dangers.
- Specific training and knowledge will be required for canoeing most of Britain's coastline. Until you have acquired such knowledge, or have a guide, stick to safe tourist areas where rescue services are operating.

Lakes

- Practise your deep water rescues and beware of the wind.
- Islands in lakes are great places to visit. You may find one suitable for camping overnight.

Basic techniques – manoeuvring

As your experience and choice of venue develop, you will learn how to manoeuvre your canoe more proficiently and precisely on the water.

Here are some manoeuvring skills you will find useful, particularly when you are in a current. The principle in all these manoeuvres is to use the waterflow or current to your advantage. Understand the physics of the waterflow around your canoe and it will help you to complete the manoeuvres proficiently and with the minimum of effort.

Reverse ferryglide manoeuvre

This is a manoeuvre that will:

- move your canoe across a current;
- slow you down to give you more time as you approach danger;
- enable you to avoid obstacles, e.g. trees or rocks.

The reverse ferryglide can also be used to glide sideways into the bank to stop. The manoeuvre requires proficient reverse paddling skills.

SUNDAY

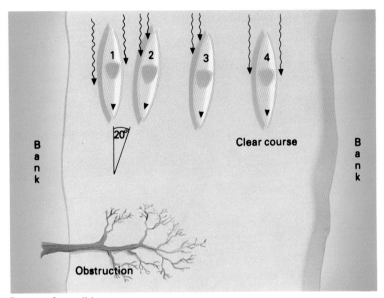

Reverse ferryglide
1 **Reverse paddle**
2 **Set the angle**
3 **Maintain the angle**
4 **Forward paddle**

Technique Tips – Reverse ferryglide

- Reverse paddle – slow down until you are stationary relative to the bank. The waterflow should be parallel with the length of your canoe.
- Continue to reverse paddle and turn your stern towards the bank, away from the obstacle you are avoiding. The waterflow will now push against the upstream side of your canoe and manoeuvre or ferryglide you away from the obstacle.
- The angle of your canoe to the waterflow is very small; no more than 20 degrees. In a stronger flow the angle needed for the manoeuvre will be less.
- Continue to reverse paddle, maintaining this angle, until you have crossed the waterflow sufficiently to continue downstream on a clear course.
- Now paddle forwards and away you go.

87

SUNDAY

Starting and stopping in a current

Some understanding of the waterflow is necessary for these manoeuvres. Wherever a strong current flows downstream, it will cause a counter-flow by the bank or anywhere in the river where the flow passes an obstruction, e.g. a rock.

The counter-flow is called an **eddy current**. The two currents can be seen clearly if you study the water.

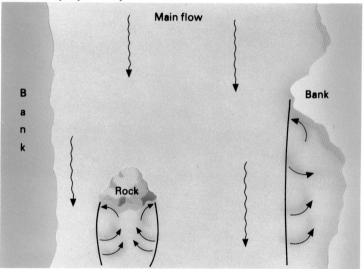

Where is the eddy current?
Canoeists use the eddy current to their advantage.

Breaking in manoeuvre

This technique is used to move out of the eddy current into the main waterflow.

Technique Tips – Breaking in

- The canoe starts in the eddy current pointing up the river.
- Forward paddle with your canoe at a slight angle to the main waterflow.
- As your bow penetrates the waterflow it will be turned down river. It is important to increase your speed before the bow enters the waterflow.
- Stability is now important – as the bow penetrates, the canoe must be tilted away from the water pressure.

Technique Tips – Breaking in – *Cont.*

If you imagine a motorbike rounding a bend, the bike will lean into the bend to maintain stability. This is what is meant by tilting. The technical term in canoeing is to edge the canoe. Bracing your knees will help you edge. The edging can be supported with a stroke called a **low brace**. The position of the paddle is similar to the low recovery stroke, but further towards the stern.

- As you break in, if more turning is required, transfer your low brace into a reverse sweep stroke.
- You should now be facing down river. Paddle forwards and away you go.

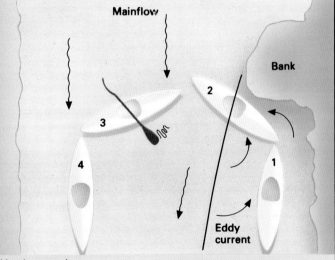

Breaking in – starting

1 Face up river in eddy	3 Low brace for support
2 Forward paddle into main flow	4 Paddle down river

Breaking out manoeuvre

Breaking out is a dynamic manoeuvre to stop your canoe continuing
down the flow by moving into an eddy current.

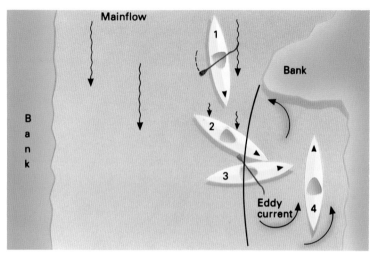

Breaking out – stopping
1 Line-up for breakout
2 Sweep stroke into eddy
3 Low brace for support
4 Stop in eddy facing up-river

Technique Tips – Breaking out

- The manoeuvre starts in the main waterflow with the canoe
  pointing down river.
- Positioning your canoe as you approach the eddy current is
  important. Paddle downstream so that as your bow passes the
  start of the eddy current, you are no more than one metre
  away.
- Forward sweep the bow into the eddy.
- Continue your forward movement edging the canoe towards
  the inside of the turn as you enter the eddy. Remember the
  motorbike.
- Stabilise your turn with a low brace.
- Reverse sweep stroke if more turning is required.
- You should now be facing up river in the eddy.

SUNDAY

With these new skills you will be able to manoeuvre safely to avoid dangers and to canoe down simple rapids.

Recording your journey

It is always worth recording the details of your journey for future reference, or maybe even your memoirs. It may be some time before your next venture.

Take particular note of:

- Equipment that was not worth taking.
- What you needed that you did not have.
- Ideas for food and menus.
- Problems or difficulties that you encountered, and how they could be overcome next time.

Your environment

Conservation is a well-used word of our time. Learn to respect your canoeing environment.

The canoe travels the waters of the world and pollutes nothing. It leaves no trace. Make sure that you are at one with your canoe.

SUNDAY

What next?

At the beginning of the book, I suggested that you would not become competent overnight; it would take time. Also that learning to canoe was all about experimenting and having fun.

I hope that now, after your journey, you are feeling more competent, that you have had some fun, and that you have enjoyed experimenting.

Most important of all, I hope that you want to do more canoeing.

There are so many journeys to make and, if you are like me, not enough time to make them.

You may be content to amble through the countryside exploring the slow-moving waterways of our island. Take your friends, take your family – to gain the most, paddle slowly.

If you thirst for more exciting adventures, there is plenty in store.

- Learn some moving water skills.
- Learn about the sea and its coastline.
- Travel abroad and visit the great water highways of the world.

Experience that special kind of freedom.

Good paddling.

GLOSSARY

aft   towards the back or stern

bivvy   a makeshift shelter
bow   the front end of a canoe
breaking in   a manoeuvre for moving from an eddy current or the bank into the main flow
breaking out   a manoeuvre for moving from the mainflow into an eddy current. The canoe turns through 180 degrees
British Canoe Union   Adbolton Lane, West Bridgford, Nottingham NG2 5AS
buoyancy aid   a flotation garment worn by anyone pursuing water sports

canoe   the collective name for open canoes and kayaks
capsize   upturning the canoe with the paddler(s) safely ejecting to the water surface
cockpit   the area around the seat of a kayak

deck   the topside of a kayak
deep water rescue   a method of righting an upturned canoe and helping the paddler(s) back inside
directional control   ability to keep the canoe on a straight course
directional stability   design feature in a canoe to keep it on a straight course
draw stroke   an effective stroke for moving the canoe sideways towards the paddle
drive face   the power side of the paddle blade. It is either flat or has a concave curve

eddy current   a counter current to the mainflow of water caused by obstructions to the flow
edge the canoe   lean the canoe to assist stability when manoeuvring in a current
end grabs   the attachment for holding onto the end of a canoe
eskimo roll   technique for self-righting a kayak

feathered   the angle set between the blades of a paddle or the angle set between the paddle blade and the water
fetch   the distance the wind or waves have travelled across the water
fibrepile   a synthetic fabric with good insulating properties
fore   towards the front or bow
forward paddling   propels the canoe forwards
freeboard   the height of the canoe out of the water

gunwhale   the uppermost line of the hull or where the hull meets the deck

headwind   a wind that is blowing against your direction of travel